# Watoto

### RAISING FUTURE LEADERS

Dedicated to the orphaned children of Uganda. Inspired by the Watoto Children's Choir.

I would like to express my sincere thanks to the many people who helped in the making of this book.  I am grateful to DaShaun Lalor, Shane Clarke, Natasha Ferber, Coletta Zenker, Mark Christie, Sharon Lalor and Curtis Heard. Special thanks to Ruth Scheffler for sound artistic advice and to Jeannine Barkhouse for generous help with layout. Thanks to Brent Smith and the staff at Watoto. I am especially grateful to my lovely husband, Dan, for his encouragement and for making it possible for me to work on this project.—B.L.M.

Library of Congress Cataloging in Publication Data
Murray, Brenda L., 1961-
Myambi's Second Chance/by Brenda L. Murray; Illustrated by Brenda L. Murray.
Summary: Orphaned and living on the streets of Kampala, Myambi and his brother Enoch get a second chance at life when they are found by the Watoto Child Care Ministry and integrated into a new home.
ISBN:  0-9735749-1-7

Published by Indelible Writing Inc.
Pioneer Park Box 20105,
Kitchener, Ontario  N2P 2B4
Canada

# Myambi's Second Chance

**WRITTEN AND ILLUSTRATED
BY BRENDA L. MURRAY**

My name is Myambi and I am seven years old.
I was living behind a charcoal shed in Kampala,
Uganda with my brother, Enoch. He is thirteen.
Enoch and I did not go to school. Most of the time
we searched for food.

Sometimes a fruit vendor would give us bruised bananas or mangoes or avocados that no one would buy. Or sometimes the Mandazi woman would give us whatever was left over at the end of the day. Mandazi is my favourite snack. It is a sweet, sugary doughnut. Sometimes Enoch worked for the charcoal seller delivering sacks of charcoal in a wheelbarrow. Then we would buy milk and day old millet bread.

We would take our feast into our shelter and watch planes flying over the city. I know exactly when a plane will pass over and which way it will go.

"Do planes fly higher than angels?" I ask Enoch.

Enoch puts his arm around me and tells me I ask too many questions. I know I am lucky to have Enoch looking after me. So many children living in the streets of Kampala have no one at all. They search for food in the garbage dump and have no one to love them.

One evening there was no work at the charcoal shed and no scraps from the Mandazi woman and no bruised fruit from the fruit vendor. We huddled together and looked for planes. I dozed off on Enoch's shoulder then woke with a start when I heard a scuffling sound.

At first I thought it was just the
rats but when I peeked out of our shelter
I saw a beautiful loaf of millet bread in our
alley. It was fresh and still warm from the oven.
"The angels are watching over us," Enoch said.
"Do angels wear red shoes?" I asked.

The next day we found another loaf of millet bread and two perfect mangoes in the alley. Every day for a week we found another gift of food which we took, of course. But we were anxious to avoid strangers because we had learned that sometimes adults can't be trusted.

One day we found our gift of fresh bread in the usual place in the alley as we had come to expect but this time our gift was in the hands of a stranger. It was being held by the lady with red shoes. She didn't appear to be going away. Enoch eyed her warily. I liked her soft eyes and her smile and her red shoes. She asked us about our parents.

Enoch told her our father was shot by the Resistance Army and then our mother became infected with HIV/AIDS. Enoch fed her and cared for her but she didn't get better.

"She is with the angels now," Enoch said.

"Have you no other relatives?" the lady asked.

We told her about our aunt who is a widow and has five young children to feed. There isn't enough food for all of us.

After our mother died Enoch said we should go to the city. There will be more food there, he thought. We walked all the way from our village to Kampala. The trip was very dangerous. We were always watching out for the Resistance Army who sometimes catch children and force them to be child soldiers. Sometimes kids just disappear. Everyone is afraid. We slept many nights in ditches and our stomachs were pinching. It was a very long way. When I got tired Enoch carried me.

The lady with the red shoes said we deserved a second chance. She asked us if we would like to go to school. She told us we could join a family of children who also have no parents.

"They all go to school," she said, "and they all have enough to eat."

The lady took us to the Watoto Children's Village. We met our new family: six other children and a nice lady named Zibia who smelled like soap. Everyone calls her Mama. She placed her hand softly on my head.

"Welcome," she said.

Mama Zibia gave us shoes and clean clothes. Then she handed me a plate full of matooke. The plantains and beef were steaming and the spices made my mouth water.

"Is it all for me?" I asked.

"Of course," she said. Then she smiled and tears spilled down her cheeks at the same time.

That first night I asked Enoch to sleep with me in my bed. It was soft and warm. I couldn't remember ever going to bed without feeling my stomach pinching. I was very sleepy but I tried to stay awake so I could see the planes cross the night sky.

"You will have to learn the new flight patterns," Enoch whispered.

"Do you think the angels know where we are?" I asked.

Our new teacher, Mr. Mutebi, says Enoch is a very good student but I must work hard to catch up with the other children my age. My reading is slow but teacher says I ask a lot of good questions and I am learning quickly.

Enoch and I have devotions with our new family. Enoch is allowed to read first because he is the oldest. We learned that God cares for us and puts his angels in charge over us. Enoch says when he grows up he wants to help children like us who have no parents.

Mama Zibia said I can be whatever I want.
"Anything?" I asked her. "Really anything?"
"The sky is the limit," she said.
I decided that I want to find out if planes fly higher than angels.
"When I grow up," I said, "I'm going to be a pilot."

Begun in 1994 by Gary and Marilyn Skinner, Watoto Child Care Ministries is a compassionate response to the orphan crisis confronting Uganda where approximately 2 million children have been orphaned as a result of civil war or the AIDS epidemic.

Watoto helps by building homes for orphaned children. They become part of a caring family of eight children and a house mother. They are provided with food and clothing, education and health care. These homes are clustered in villages that include a primary school, high school, water project, medical clinic and church/community centre.

Here children are nurtured and loved and given a second chance at life. They learn that they are valued and have something important to contribute to their community and to our world.

Consider the alternative. In another decade those 2 million orphaned children who survive their life on the streets will have grown up unloved, uneducated, and angry. But thanks to organizations like Watoto Child Care Ministries many of these children can experience a life that is much different. This crisis is desperate.

Won't you consider how you can help raise Uganda's future leaders?

All proceeds from the sale of this book, less the costs, will be used to care for orphaned children in WATOTO CHILD CARE MINISTRIES UGANDA. If you have received this book as a gift, please consider sending a donation to one of the addresses below so that other children like Myambi and Enoch will have a home, food, clean clothes, health care and be able to go to school.

WATOTO CHILD CARE MINISTRIES U.S.A.
PO Box 1320
Lutz, FL
U.S.A.  33548-1320

WATOTO CHILD CARE MINISTRIES AUSTRALIA
PO Box 2632
Mansfield DC
Australia QLD 4122

WATOTO CHILD CARE MINISTRIES CANADA
PO Box 98
Victoria, BC
V8W 2M1

WATOTO CHILD CARE MINISTRIES U.K.
PO Box 690
Dagenham, Essex
UK  RM9 5YZ

www.watoto.com

Brenda L. Murray is a writer and artist who lives in Ontario, Canada with her husband, Dan, and children Peter, Kaitlin and Danielle. She is a member of The Writer's Guild of Canada.

Also written and illustrated by Brenda L. Murray:
The Great Canadian Car Camping Cookbook